A SCENE
IN BETWEEN

TRIPPING THROUGH THE FASHIONS
OF UK INDIE MUSIC 1980 – 1988

For Violet and Herbie, my blitzkrieg boppers

Sam Knee and friend / '84
In a Camden cafe waiting for the Gun Club/Scientists gig at the
Electric Ballroom.

2

Dive Into Yesterday
An Introduction

The generation that came of age via the underground scenes of the '80s, sandwiched between the new wave and grunge, has been largely brushed over, written out of history in favour of the more familiar territories that bookend either side of the decade. '81-'88 was a golden age for the UK's indie guitar scenes – a moment in which '60s folk garage rock combined with late '70s punk rock in an unlikely sonic alliance that signified a brief return to DIY culture. Punk's last gasp if you like. *A Scene In Between* sets out to excavate the sartorial treasures of this UK indie youth scenery spanning; Postcard via Whaam! and Creation records, *C86*, garage punk, shoegaze and the multifarious micro sub-scenes that sprouted in between. It's by no means an '80s indie who's who, purely a glimpse into the visual racket of the era and all its canoodlings. Mode over music.

My musical rites of passage occurred aged 15. Up to that point, I hadn't discovered anything I felt a genuine affinity with. I had dabbled with the mod revival, as it looked sharp, but largely found the bands of the movement uninspiring, conservative and at times a bit laddy, which for a gangly, withdrawn wimp like myself was a non-starter. Plus I grew tired of being called a plastic. Then one fine day my sister brought home a copy of the latest Cramps album, *Psychedelic Jungle*. From her room I could hear the delicious, syrupy dirge of "Green Fuz" oozing out from under the door and was compelled to venture closer... I had to see who was behind this bedlam. Intrigued further by their cryptic Hammer Horror sleeve and the possibility that I was holding something 'psychedelic' – a word I had always been fascinated by – I was sold.

With my newfound obsession, I embarked on finding out all and everything. I joined the fan club 'Legion of the Cramped', my friend Steve dyed my hair black, borrowed some crimpers from a girl at school, picked up a pair of Shelley's Chelsea boots, drainpipe black jeans, an old black leather box jacket and underwent a revolt into style with a more scruffy, punky '60s look.

The Cramps, for me, were the dawning of everything, luring me to distant musical shores. The discovery that a vast proportion of their repertoire was actually obscure '50s and '60s cover versions led me to seek out and savour the delights of the originals via compilations like *Nuggets*, *Pebbles* and the never-ending bottomless pit of '60s garage punk and psychedelia and beyond. This was the celestial path that brought me to the '80s/'60s crossover indie scenes that form the foundation of this book. Others got there via post-punk, mod revival roots, goth or some were just plain born indie.

It's easy to understand why so many young folk (myself included) felt disconnected from the times they were living in and were seduced by the poetic paisley haze and noisy positive moxie of an era rich with romanticism and escapism, rather than endure the ghastly, harsh, mundane reality of '80s Thatcher Britain. Micro scenes blossomed all over the UK from the darkest recesses of armpit towns, provincial coffins and the sprawling suburbs of the nation's cities, as students and largely unemployed alienated youths gravitated towards each other. These scenesters were outfitted, for the most part, in a mish mash of '50s and '60s second hand clothes which were still readily available for pennies from charity shops, jumble sales and flea markets – that's if you were willing to sift through all the horrendous '70s fashion crime leftovers which littered the land. This was a subtle subversive reaction and rejection against the clichéd yuppie flamboyance as purveyed by the mainstream. The scene had no regional boundaries, although Scotland had the seemingly effortless capability to produce one classic band after another. Something in the water I guess?

The schmutter ingredients within these pages are an undefined, shambolic fusion of second hand finds and '80s contemporary thrown together to create an oddly beautiful vision of style. Reacting against the post-punk overcoat-wearing doom and gloomists, this new wave flaunted '50s and '60s Americana classics with some foppish English bohemia / public school type chic chucked in with careless abandon, topped off with boyish charm and a floppy fringe.

Head on style collisions somewhere between the Subway Sect's schoolboy urchin punk rocker getups and a kitchen sink period art student / CND protester type was another strand to the scene's sartorial diversity; brown corduroy blazers, '60s anoraks from our childhoods and desert boots. All reminiscent of the youth vogue featured in Vernon Richard's book, *Protest Without Illusions*, focusing on the CND (Campaign for Nuclear Disarmament) marches in the UK throughout the late '50s, early '60s.

Velvet Underground inspired attire, particularly the de rigueur of John Cale or Sterling Morrison circa '66/'67 was also popular; blackened jeans on skinny gangly legs, Chelsea or engineer boots, a fine gauge knit black roll neck sweater, rounded off with a fantastically manicured moppish lampshade full-face-covering bowl haircut. The ubiquitous black leather box jacket went with all the above. A noticeable spin-off from this was the leather trouser phenomena usually associated with the Creation Records roster (or for those with rockist leanings, perhaps an ironic gesture gone haywire), which a couple of contributors have referenced as being rooted in Hamburg-era Fab-Four. Of course, not everyone wanted to look like they were in the Byrds circa '65, but it was a youth fashion trend that existed peaking between '85 to '87. Amalgamate any of the above in any random combination and a '80s/'60s indie Shangri La metamorphosis was spawned.

It's also worth noting the vast deluge of mainly bootleg compilation LPs of obscure '60s beat, garage and psychedelic sounds that became hugely popular across the youth scenes throughout the decade. Previously little known bands from the mid to late '60s became commonly known amongst this new generation. Most indie clubs in the '80s played a mix of contemporary sounds you could bowl out to plus a few old punk rock faves as well integrating a fair dose of '60s garage and mod beat quite naturally into the mix. From working in record shops throughout the '80s, I can attest that it was fairly standard practice to sell, for example, a Primal Scream or Pastels single, along with a Love or 13th Floor Elevators reissue LP and a Ramones or X Ray-Spex album all in the same transaction. Such was the capacious kaleidoscopic musical landscape of the era.

I decided to end this story in '88, when the scenes featured here began to fade and the ghastly advent of all things 'baggy' approached. I took a step back to a mid '60s groundhog day where skinny was always in, which for the most part is where I still reside. This "Psychedelic Journey Parts One" to quote The Mystic Tide is made up of photos contributed from archives from original scenesters, fans, band members, fanzine editors, bedroom label folk and budding photographers from the time – all

taken before the dream faded and where the rainbow ends. All, bar a handful, are previously unpublished. I wanted to produce something genuine, from the inside looking out, not just some poseur peering in. And I hope this comes across, as it is my intent, my aim is true.

I would like to add in one disclaimer: The term 'indie' is generally despised by all (myself included). But I was torn on what to use as an alternative subtitle that would be internationally recognisable by fashion/ music fans alike, so after much toing and froing, it stuck.

Oh, and by the way... *A Scene In Between* doesn't die here. A further volume featuring international indie icons is a distinct possibility so please continue sending your '80s indie pics through to me at *www.asceneinbetween.com*. Be part of the scene, not part of the scenery!

Lastly, if you're tired of your '60s/'80s indie record collections clogging up your life then feel free drop me a line and I'll relieve you of your vinyl burdens. You can thank me later.

– Sam Knee

Orange Juice / '80
Glasgow's premier indie pop outfit: Edwyn Collins, James
Kirk, David McClymont. The original photo for their "Falling
and Laughing" debut single and first release on the seminal
Postcard Records label. An image of monolithic proportions
that launched thousands of floppy fringes and kick-started
the '80s 'indie pop' revolution.

Edwyn Collins / '81
Postcard Records' pin-up boy.

Orange Juice / '81
Live at The Spaghetti Factory, Glasgow.

Left: Edwyn Collins / '82
Live at Bristol University.

Above: Orange Juice / '81
Steven Daly, James Kirk, David McClymont, Edwyn Collins.

Above: Edwyn Collins / '81

Right: Philip King / 81'
Post The Beautiful Loser, later of The Servants and Felt.

"We would to go to jumble sales to buy old clothes, annuals and records. My blazer and lumberjack shirt were American in origin and came from Flip, a recently opened shop in Long Acre, Covent Garden that sold old clothing stock that had been shipped over in bulk from the US – a very new concept in the UK. The trousers were a pair of old cricket ones." – Philip King

Above: James Kirk / '81

Right: Davy Henderson of the Fire Engines / '80
Seminal Edinburgh-based the Fire Engines were named after a
13th Floor Elevators' song. The band's early shows were a minimal,
noisy blitz on the crowd. Live at Rock Garden, London.

*"The Fire Engines… fantastic, they used to play for 25 minutes at
the most… And you see loads of groups playing for 45-50 minutes
and you just get bored after 25."* – Bobby Gillespie in Raygun
fanzine, '85.

Left: Gina Davidson of Marine Girls / '81
Hertford teenage indie pop quartet, Marine Girls, were formed by
Gina Davidson and Tracey Thorn (later of Everything but the Girl)
while they were still in the sixth form at school. Their classic low
fi (or no fi?) *Beach Party* album was recorded in a shed in Ilford.
A seminal act, their influence has been cited by many including
Talulah Gosh, Beat Happening and Kurt Cobain. Along with Dolly
Mixture, the Marine Girls pioneered the indie girl fashion look that
followed on through the rest of the decade and beyond.

Above: Marine Girls / '81
Gina Davidson, Alice Fox on vox, Jane Fox, live at Buntingford
Fire Station.

BENEFIT CONCERT FOR THE HERTFORD
★ COMMUNITY/ARTS CENTRE ★
T.V. PERSONALITIES ★
★ INFINITE LOTS ★
ELUSIVE DIPLOMATS
MARINE GIRLS ★
WEDNESDAY MAY 6TH
7·30 PM
Balls Park College, Main Hall.
Admission £1·00
(50p with a Dole card.)

Left: Gina Davidson, Gillian Elam and Dan Treacy / '81
This photo was taken in Chelsea whilst some students shot a promo film for the "Smashing Time" single, which remains lost in time. Gina Davidson with duffle bag, Gillian Elam, who was involved with the cassette label Bi-Joopiter Expression, and Dan Treacy, songwriting genius and founding member of seminal art-pop pioneers, Television Personalities. Treacy's Whaam! Records released the Marine Girls' LP, *Beach Party*, later reissued on Cherry Red.

Right top: Gina and pals / '81

Right bottom: Flyer / '81
Designed by future Television Personality, Mark Flunder.

Previous page: Paradise Now / '81
Ken Copsey, Andy Crathern, Mick Bacon and Mick O'Mara.
Early Captain Beefheart inspired teen garage, Hastings.

Above left: Debsey Wykes of Dolly Mixture / '81
Cambridge post-punk girl pop trio.

Above right: Rachel Bor of Dolly Mixture / '81

Right: The Delmontes / '81
Edinburgh-based psych-ish ensemble. Drummer Bernice Simpson
(far left) went on to play with The Pastels a few years later.

This page: John Robb / '85
John Robb, ace indie face on the scenes and
member of Blackpool's post punk noize racketeers,
The Membranes. Robb was also mastermind of
DIY fanzine, *Rox*.

Right top: Jill Bryson of Strawberry Switchblade / '81
In her art school days, Glasgow.

Right bottom: Velda Pond / '87
Indie scenester in her room in Southend-on-Sea, Essex.

Paul Haig of Josef K / '80
Edinburgh-based band that signed to Alan Horne's visionary
Postcard Records along with Orange Juice, and became a
key component in "The Sound of Young Scotland". They were
dark, existential and didn't play encores. Live in Glasgow.

Stephen Pastel and Jill Bryson / '82
Stephen pre-mop fringe and anorak, sporting a duffle coat and DMs
ensemble. In Glasgow with Jill of Strawberry Switchblade.

Glasgow's The Pastels are probably the main reason the book you're holding came about, as I felt their music and sartorial style were the logical progression that bridged the gap from post-punk into the new '80s indie era. Releasing their debut single, "Songs For Children", on Whaam! The Pastels sounded somewhere between the Television Personalities, Swell Maps, early Red Crayola and the Velvet Underground… they made a precious racket indeed.

Stephen Pastel also became something of a fashion icon, although when asked in issue 5 of *Slow Dazzle* fanzine from '84 what his thoughts were on fashion, he replied, "I don't really know about fashion at all. I can't be bothered spending a lot of money on clothes, I just like to put on things that are amusing, pleasing to wear and comfortable."

The Pastels / '82
Early shot of The Pastels performing live with Strawberry Switchblade at The Venue, Glasgow. Strawberry Switchblade sing the backing vocals on the Rough Trade single "I Wonder Why".

Previous page: The Pastels / '85
Stephen Pastel, Brian (Superstar) Taylor, Bernice Simpson and
Martin Hayward at the London Shell Building. Stephen Pastel was
at the vanguard of the '60s unisex anorak trend.

Above and right: Stephen Pastel / '86

Stephen Pastel / '86
Live at the Onion Cellar, Edinburgh.

*"We had a connection with Dan (Treacy). When The Pastels started
I could think of nothing better than being on Whaam!, which
was the TV Personalities' label. We also loved Rough Trade so we
sent tapes off to Rough Trade and Whaam! and they both really
liked our group even though we were incredibly raw and basic
and almost childlike in some ways. Dan wrote back saying he
would put out a single, and "Songs For Children" became our
first release. I went to London and met Dan and he was such a
sweet kid at the time. He had such pale, beautiful skin and I was
freaked out that he was so young, yet had been part of that first
wave of punk. Dan was probably only two or three years older
than me but he had already done all this stuff." – Stephen Pastel
interview on thequietus.com, 2013*

Above and right: The Pastels / '86

A sartorial ramble with bohemian style icon Stephen Pastel

SK: In the early '80s you pioneered the look that became synonymous with indie music fans – the anorak, '60s art school style hair, etc. Where did this look stem from? Was there a direct influence?

SP: I never really felt I had one particular look, it was more a mixture of things which changed through time. When the group started I was quite young and really just trying to establish an identity for myself. I wasn't really sure what it was, but I knew I didn't feel a particular need to join in with all the post-punk styles, and the alternative in Glasgow was a tendency towards slightly preppy-looking '50s Americana. I never really wanted to look like an American, and my influences were more British / European, although there was also part of me that wanted to look like I didn't belong to a particular country or place or year. I really tried to make things up for myself but my ideal was probably a sort of anti-glamour glamour, like the way Jane Asher looks when she's hitch-hiking in *Alfie*. Or to think of someone in music, I liked the way Epic Soundtracks from Swell Maps looked ... quite understated, with slightly scruffy but well-chosen clothes and a loose haircut.

I liked new clothes that were intrinsically good but unfashionable; Marks & Spencer's V-neck sweaters, Clarks shoes, brown cords. If it was raining, an anorak was ok, and in winter, a dufflecoat. You could really put a good look together from all these things and with odd bits of second hand too. At the time I think I felt a bit isolated but then I started to meet up with other isolated people and we probably started to influence each other and our own styles combined into more of a look. You know, Annabel (Aggi) was really cool and we cut each other's hair and she was just so uncompromising and original. We were often just zeroing out from our own time, trying to make up our own styles, which were sometimes a bit childlike or raw, but sometimes really came together.

SK: You emerged at a point in time where there seemed to be little else going on and most of the best bands had either broken up or had gone off the boil and lost all relevance. Who inspired you at the time to form a band?

SP: Well, I think if we considered it, we felt in some way that we were a bit out of time or that we'd arrived too late. On the surface, music seemed to have become more aspirational, more hi-fi shop demo. That was our impression in Glasgow anyway. We were quite raw and basic, but to an extent we fitted in with the culture of cassette swapping and fanzines. At the time, groups like Television Personalities and The Fall were really strong and something to look up to. We became friends with Strawberry Switchblade and then started to meet other like-minded people. But at first there wasn't so much, and I really think that was the best time to start out because we weren't joining in before we had something of our own.

SK: Throughout my research I've asked various people who they think spearheaded the whole leather trouser look that became synonymous with all Creation bands. Your name has frequently been the answer. Were you aware at the time that you were responsible for a guitar band sub-fashion movement?

SP: I was given a pair of leather trousers and I thought they would look quite subversive without, you know, the cliches of rock and roll. So my favourite look for a while was in combination with this late '60s-styled brown cord jacket which I'd had made. I liked a lot of browns and blacks, and I suppose I was sometimes trying to juxtapose odd things and look kind of

cool. I don't know if I was one of the first people from that time to wear leather trousers, I probably was. Other people went more rock and roll with their look so I really never felt that they were taking their cues from me.

SK: In the '80s where did you use to buy clothes? Did you have any fave shops or markets?

SP: I was often looking for old stock in slightly off-the-beaten-track oddball shops. There was a great one along Dumbarton Road in Partick, which was definitely not for the faint-hearted. Oxfam shops in posh areas, Paddy's Market now and then. But like I say, I often just shopped in Marks & Spencer or the Co-operative or Hoey's (a local retailer).

SK: What was your most treasured item of clothing back then?

SP: I can't really remember, I tried not to get too stuck on things. I liked the cord jacket that I'd had made, it was a really good look for me.

SK: What do you think about being regarded as a indie music fashion icon?

SP: Well, it's ironic, I always hated the word 'indie' and if I'm truthful I hated a lot of the music that came to be called indie. But independent music in its originality and oddness offered me something that was my only possibility in terms of what I wanted to do, which was make music with like-minded people. I always tried my best to be original both in music and, although it's less important to me now, in the way I looked. So of course it's flattering if someone sees me as being an iconic part of something that has a cultural significance.

Above left: Flyer / '86
Pastels and Vaselines flyer, The Venue, Glasgow.

Above right: Stephen Pastel / '84
In a Glasgow subway.

Overleaf left: Dan Treacy / '82
Founding member of the Television Personalities and of Whaam!
Records. The influence of post part-time punk veterans, the
Television Personalities, on the burgeoning wave of UK rackety
jangle was undeniably paramount. Similarly, without Whaam!
there may never have been Creation (or at least as we know it).
Note the copy of "Mummy, You're Not Watching Me" in the top left.

Overleaf top right: Dan Treacy / '85
At the Room at the Top, Dan's club above the Enterprise pub,
Chalk Farm, London.

Overleaf bottom right: Dan Treacy / '82

Left: Dan Treacy and Jowe Head of the Television Peronalities / '84
Taken on the last ever night of The Living Room club, hosted by
Alan McGee – founder of Creation Records. Incidentally, two TVPs
tracks from this night are featured on the *Alive In The Living Room*
compilation, the first album release on Creation Records.

Above: Dave Musker and Joe Foster of the TVPs / '84

Overleaf: *Slow Dazzle* **/ '84**
Original cover artwork for the sixth and final issue of the superb
Greenock-based fanzine *Slow Dazzle*, the brainchild of Chris
Davidson, a mover and shaker in the area. Spot the naughty words
hidden within.

(THE FINAL REPORT)
NEIL YOUNG
THE LEGEND!
JOHN PEEL
CREATION RECORDS
KURT VONNEGUT
ary Chain
PAT NEVIN
A CERTAIN RATIO

East Kilbride's the Jesus and Mary Chain were apparently named after a free gift in a cereal packet. Their early shows were a riotous racket and soon stuff of legend. "Upside Down", released on Alan McGee's fledgling Creation label, was unarguably one of the defining moments of the decade, with huge blown out walls of fuzz distortion and feedback hitherto only found in the more extreme ends of the punk scenes. The melodic, yet apathetic vocals were buried in a shallow grave within the overwhelming din. Coupled with a skull crushing dirge-like adaptation of Syd Barrett's "Vegetable Man", the single was an amphetamine-fueled youth noize pop masterpiece. The band at this stage also looked cool as shit in their '60s beat via Subway Sect threads and made everyone else suddenly seem like old farts.

Above: Jesus and Mary Chain / '85
Bobby Gillespie, Douglas Hart, William Reid. Live at Ziggy's, Plymouth.

Right top and bottom: JAMC / '85
The band with manager Alan McGee, top picture far right.

Previous page left: JAMC / '84
Jim Reid and Douglas Hart at the Ambulance Station, Old Kent
Road, London.

Previous page right: Jim Reid / '84

Above: Jim Reid / '84
At the Ambulance Station, London.

Right: Bobby Gillespie / '84

The JAMC leather-boy visual aesthetic was arguably inspired by rocker youth street fashion of the early '60s. A key influence was the book *Rock and Roll Times* by photographer Jurgen Vollmer, published in '82. The book featured pictures of the Beatles in their pre-mop-top, black-leather clad Gene Vincent phase, as well as images of Vollmer and his friends, who were somberly dressed art school beatniks – scruffy early modernists, known then as 'Exi's', short for existentialists.

Left: Douglas Hart / '84

Above left: William Reid / '85

Above right: Jim Reid and Bobby Gillespie / '85

Overleaf: JAMC / '84
The Ambulance Station, Old Kent Road, London. An infamous gig, which after loosely performing five songs, descended into pandemonium.

Above: JAMC / '85
Bobby on drums, William Reid feeding back. Feel the noize.
Live at Ziggy's, Plymouth.

*"JAMC came out on stage around midnight to an air high
anticipation and just killed it for a little over 20 minutes. Loud and
fucked up feedback. Bobby was just playing a single drum in a
skinny blue '60s crew neck. Douglas was stoic on bass and Jim
was screaming and tripping over William crouched at his amp.
It was over so fast I was lucky to sneak a few photos on my
primitive camera. My ears rang for days. There was no riot other
than the riot of noise…. The impact and memory of the show is
still with us to this day." – Photographer James Finch*

Right: JAMC / '85
Performing for a Belgian television show.

Michael Kerr and Eddie Connelly of Meat Whiplash / '85
East Kilbride's Meat Whiplash's trebled out "Don't Slip Up" is one
of the finest noise pop records of the decade and a defining
moment of the early Creation releases.

*"The original line-up of Meat Whiplash included Douglas Hart on
guitar but he went off to join the Jesus and Mary Chain. Our links
with the Mary Chain actually went back years. Eddie had been
friends with Jim Reid for ages and Douglas was also a friend. I
think they felt a mutual understanding with us, coming from the
same shitty town and from the same type of background. The Mary
Chain were a product of high unemployment at the time as were
Meat Whiplash. We formed a band out of boredom as much as
anything else, looking for anything that would break the monotony
of an unemployed or unemployable existence.*

*Around this time the Jesus and Mary Chain were getting some
success and asked us to support them in Glasgow, this was our
first gig and I think we played four songs, two originals and two
covers. We were then asked to support them at North London
Polytechnic. In the aftermath of that infamous gig, Alan McGee
came running into the dressing room, declared "we've got to do a
single" and left the room as quickly as he had entered.*

*Fashion-wise it was a bit of a mix, the Hamburg-era Beatles
always looked cool and the black jumpers worn by quite a lot of
us at that time were often knitted by my mother, not very rock and
roll but true nonetheless. I think the jumpers worn by Jim Reid and
Douglas Hart on The Old Grey Whistle Test were also made by my
mother." – Michael Kerr*

Left and above: Pete Astor of The Weather Prophets / '85
London band The Weather Prophets evolved out of The Loft, who
were originally called The Living Room, who were regulars at Alan
McGee's club of the same name (confusing, huh?). More cool
Creation jangle in a Velvets, Television vein.

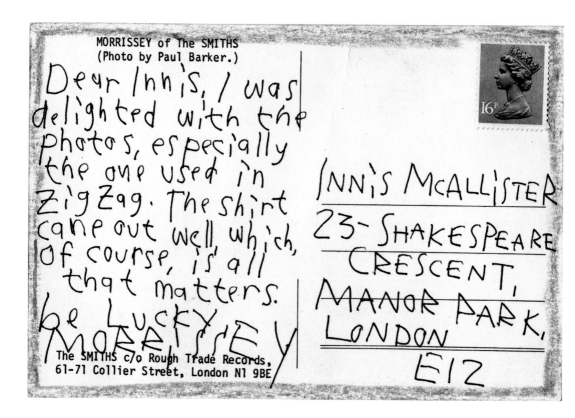

MORRISSEY of The SMITHS
(Photo by Paul Barker.)

Dear Innis, I was delighted with the photos, especially the one used in ZigZag. The shirt came out well which, of course, is all that matters. be Lucky MORRISSEY

The SMITHS c/o Rough Trade Records, 61-71 Collier Street, London N1 9BE

INNIS McALLISTER
23- SHAKESPEARE
CRESCENT,
MANOR PARK,
LONDON
E12

Above: Message from Morrissey / '84
Postcard penned by Morrissey to photographer Innis McAllister.

Right: *Zigzag Magazine* / '84
Morrissey on the back cover of the magazine, wearing the shirt
mentioned in the postcard. Live at a free GLC benefit gig,
South Bank, London.

In the spring of 1984 I booked an eye test at a local opticians in
Southend after discovering they still stocked original '60s NHS frames
left over from the time, exactly like the ones Morrissey was sporting.
Sadly, I was well and truly brassic. However, being a new sign-up as
one of 'Maggies millions' all I had to do was fail the eye test to bag the
specs for free. Sitting down awkwardly in the test chair and squinting
as the test cards came up, I deliberately flunked each question. My
atrocious test results confirmed my medical need for spectacles and
a week later I was able to collect a pair of the classic '60s frames. I
strolled out of the opticians, immediately putting the glasses on and
admiring the distorted view in a shop window. The look I had been
hankering for was finally complete as I triumphantly promenaded down
the high street. The migraine that followed was of little significance as
a degree of pain for fashion was a given thing and quite natural in my
opinion. How I looked and the music I listened to was the only thing of
importance. SK

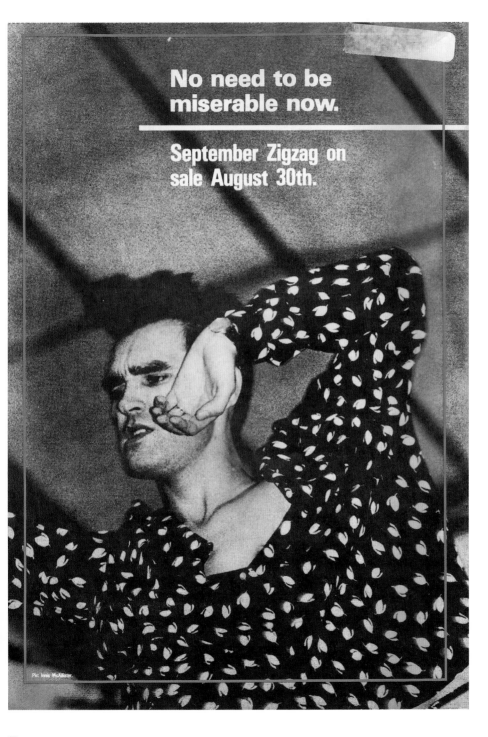

No need to be
miserable now.

September Zigzag on
sale August 30th.

Pic: Innis McAllister.

How important are clothes to you? *They don't have the relevance they once had, like in the '60s you could look at someone and assess their personality. That's not the case anymore. Clothes are no longer the window of the soul.*

OK. So is style important? *Style has nothing to do with clothes. You can't become stylish; either you are or you aren't. But you can become fashionable. You can go out and buy the stuff. But again, if you wear it badly it means nothing.*
— Morrissey Interview for I-D *Magazine, Feb '83*

Susan, This piece of paper is not terribly inspiring, as you know. And so:

MORRISSEY xxxx

Its awful when your entire life revolves around the 10:05 train to Arbroath.

Above: Postcard / '84

Another note penned by Morrissey featuring self-portrait to loyal fan, Susan Henderson.

Previous page, right and overleaf: The Smiths / September '83
Andy Rourke, Mike Joyce, Morrissey, Johnny Marr. A series of early Smiths snaps taken by Martin Whitehead at the Moles Club, Bath, which have been languishing in a box in negative form for 30 years and have never seen the light of day until now.

"On the strength of nothing more than their first single, "Hand In Glove", I wanted to interview The Smiths for my fanzine, The Underground. *My usual method of turning up at the venue at sound check time when the band might be hanging around with time to spare worked again, and I got one of the best interviews of my fanzine career. Moles Club back then could hold maybe 100 people. There wasn't even room for a stage. Despite that, the club was about two-thirds empty. Barely 30 people had turned up. Five months later The Smiths played to a packed out main hall at Bristol University. I couldn't even get close to the stage, never mind the band." – Martin Whitehead*

Previous page left: The Servants / '85
Philip King, John Mohan, John Wills, David Westlake. Cool
and refined indie with a Velvety nonchalance.

Previous page right: Sam Knee and sister, Sarah / '85
Thru the flowers – at home in Leigh-on-Sea. Suburban
bliss.

Left: James Endeacott / '83
Endeacott later became the guitarist of psychedelic
proto-shoegaze masters, Loop. Kicking back in Exmouth.

Above: The House of Love / '86
Guy Chadwick, Chris Groothuizen, Andrea Heukamp.
Lysergic emanations from Camberwell. Live at the Black
Horse, Camden.

Above: Phil Wilson and Simon Beesley of The June Brides / '85

Right: Phil Wilson and Simon Beesley / '83
Post-punk inspired indie pop, The June Brides, performing their
first ever gig at The Spotted Cow, Lewisham.

The Dentists / '85
Bob Collins, Ian Smith and Mark Matthews.
Medway's finest garage janglers psych out at
the bandstand, Victoria Gardens, Chatham.

Left: Mick Geoghegan of Mighty Mighty / '85
Birmingham's Mighty Mighty. Fine purveyors of the breezy
jingle jangle pop sound, falling somewhere between Orange
Juice and The Smiths. At Midlands Art Centre, Birmingham.

Above: Mighty Mighty / '85
Russell Burton and Hugh McGuinness.

**Right: Stephen Pastel, Alasdair (driver), The Legend
(Everett True), David Keegan / '85**
Outside Rough Trade, Talbot Road, Notting Hill.

Overleaf: Shop Assistants / '85
Sarah Kneale, Ann Donald, Laura MacPhail, Alex Taylor, David
Keegan. Live at Dan Treacy's Room at The Top club, above the
Enterprise pub, Chalk Farm, London.

The band originally called Buba and the Shop Assistants released
the sublime "Something To Do" single on Stephen Pastel's cool
Villa21 Records. They later shortened their name and replaced Aggi
(Annabel Wright), later of the Pastels, with Alex Taylor on vocals,
and released the classic *All Day Long* EP on Subway. They threw out
fast, fresh, sparkling two-minute punky pop songs with buzzing,
tinny Ramoneiac guitar riffage from '80s indie-boy style leader
David Keegan, decked out in trademark stripy jumper, skinny jeans,
sneakers, anorak and '60s schoolboy mop hair. David, Stephen
Pastel and Sandy McLean formed the indie record label 53rd and
3rd, named after the super tuff Ramones number.

Above: Shop Assistants / '85

Right: Shop Assistants / '85
Live at Mission Club, Bristol.

"When you're tired and tattered, we are all that ever mattered."
— Alex Taylor and David Keegan

Previous page left: Laura MacPhail of the Shop Assistants / '85

Previous page right: David Keegan of the Shop Assistants / '85

Above: Martin Whitehead of The Flatmates / '88
Bristol pop quartet The Flatmates, formed by Martin Whitehead,
who was also proprietor of the Subway Records Organisation label,
home of the Shop Assistants, Soup Dragons, Clouds, Razorcuts and
other crucial indie pop releases. Martin, in true DIY tradition, ran
the label from his flat in Bath and was also namedropped in the
Pooh Sticks song "On Tape": *"I sent for the Soup Dragons single,
mail order only. £1.30 to Martin Whitehead, but it never ca-ame!"*

Right: Debbie Haynes of The Flatmates / '87
Live at Dingwalls, London.

**Above: Kevin McMahon and Andrew Tully of Jesse Garon and the
Desperadoes / '87**
Edinburgh band Jesse Garon and the Desperadoes released some
effortlessly cool jangly records with West Coast '60s overtones on
the Nardonic label. The band allegedly took their name from Elvis
Presley's stillborn twin brother, Jesse Garon Presley. Live at The
Onion Cellar, Edinburgh.

Above top: Fran Schoppler, Stuart Clarke and Angus McPake of
Jesse Garon and the Desperadoes / '87

Above bottom: Andrew Tully and Margarita Vasquez-Ponte of
Jesse Garon and the Desperadoes / '87

Above: David Callahan and Muriel Pavledis / '83
David Callahan of The Wolfhounds with friend Muriel Pavledis
in Gidea Park, Essex.

Right: David Callahan of The Wolfhounds / '84
Angular indie racket with mod-ish leanings from Havering.
Live at the Clarendon Hotel, Hammersmith, London.

Shooting the breeze with Amelia Fletcher, Talulah Gosh

SK: When you first formed the band in '85, what were your influences and inspirations in a fashion sense?

AF: Probably mostly Dolly Mixture and the Marine Girls. At that point I was wearing lots of '50s clothes, similar to Tracey Thorn. It evolved, and eventually I developed more my own style but certainly it started as that. Most of my clothes were second hand from charity shops, apart from shoes, pants, bra and turtle neck jumpers from British Home Stores.

I was really into '60s music at the time – soul and girl group music. As Talulah Gosh went on, we gradually got more into that style clothes wise – geometric patterns and such.

SK: Did you evolve from more of a mod or punk background?

AF: More straight out and out indie. Postcard, and Orange Juice in particular, were one of the first things I really loved. Before that I was obsessed with Altered Images…. I guess Clare Grogan was a clothes inspiration as well. When I was a big fan of her I literally wore exactly what she wore… litte halter neck tops and ra-ra skirts.

SK: How did you end up hooking up and signing to 53rd and 3rd?

AF: The Pastels were my absolute favourite band at that time. I heard the second Pastels single, "Something Going On", on the evening BBC radio. I taped it and played it on a walkman that was running too slow and Stephen's usually drooly voice was even more drooly. I thought it was totally fantastic. I eventually heard it at the right speed, but from that moment they became my favourite band. It is only been recently that I can walk up to Stephen and talk to him quite sensibly. If someone feels kind of godlike to you, even if they haven't done anything musically that feels as godlike to you for some time, you still feel nervous.

I knew Stephen had set up 53rd and 3rd, but I've always underated how good, I guess, anything I do is…. and also not expected anyone to like it… so I didn't expect he would put it out. We knew the Subway people a bit, in fact Martin Whitehead was at our first gig in Oxford. They invited us to go and play in Bristol. Word was getting around about us remarkably fast. Somehow we had very well chosen first and second gigs which all the scenesters were at. I made a tape which had a plasticine steam train on the front, I made three copies and sent them to 53rd and 3rd, Subway and Creation. Subway came back really fast and said "yes, yes, yes", and so we said we would go with Subway for the first record.... But then Stephen Pastel rang up, and I thought "oh my goodness, Stephen Pastel does actually want to do it" so I blew out Subway, which I still feel a bit guilty about... but the fact was that my hero wanted to put my record out.

It turned out he didn't seem to have a great deal to do with the label, it was mainly run by Sandy McLean. It was a fine label with really fine bands, and Stephen's role seemed to be to identify the bands who should be on it. We ended up falling out with Sandy as we thought he wasn't giving us any money when we should be rich. He told us we hadn't made any money, and now I realise he was probably telling the truth. We were doing alright and actually we sold quite a lot of singles, but you don't make a lot of money from singles. He paid for us to record in great studios. We recorded in the studios where the Specials recorded "Ghost Town" which I don't think was particularly cheap.

SK: Throughout my research I have been trying to identify the person that started the whole anorak look.

AF: I would say either Stephen Pastel or Bobby Gillespie. Both of them were doing it in this weird way, combining them with leather trousers. I think what it was about was playing with childish imagery, very much in touch with your childish side, wearing this anorak, which is a bit twee and deliberately naïve, with leather trousers which say 'haha not really'.

When I was finishing school, Creation was kind of everything. I had the first ten singles on Creation... that was all I was listening to... it was very important to me.

I would steal away to London on the Oxford Tube (the coach service from Oxford to Marble Arch) to see Creation gigs at the Room at the Top. Creation bands did seem to popularise the leather trousers look. I certainly adopted the Creation look. I guess Talulah Gosh may have been the first to combine it with skirts. Badges were an important part of the times.

SK: How do you feel when people cite you as an indie girl fashion icon?

AF: I guess I like it, but I do feel a little naughty as I nicked most of my ideas from other people.... But maybe that's true of most people.

SK: Your name is often mentioned as inspiring the next generation on, the Riot Girl scene, both musically and sartorially.

AF: Riot Girl was as a really interesting look, as it drew on the indie style and combined it with punk and a '50s American clothes aesthetic. There was a lot of playing around with female stereotypes in the fashion of Riot Girl, which I thought was really good fun, regardless of the music or the politics.

SK: The indie scenes were mostly male dominated in the '80s. You seemed to spearhead the unisex girl aspect.

AF: My favourite bands have always had girls in them. The Pastels were originally three lads and a female drummer. Aggi appeared on a single and I said to them, "it's so much better when Aggi is involved", so it came to be. I don't know if I was influential. Dolly Mixture and Marine Girls were all girl groups. I've always liked bands more when they've had girls involved. Talulah Gosh was meant to be an all girl band, but we couldn't find enough of them.

Left: Talulah Gosh / '86
Elizabeth Price, Amelia Fletcher, Chris Scott, Peter Momtchiloff, Matthew Fletcher. Oxford-based quintet described by journalist and musician The Legend (whose "73 in 83" single was the first release on Creation) as, "glorious strands of classic pop/noise a la Pastels/ Mary Chain coated with an irresistible covering of two female voices".

Above: Amelia Fletcher / '87

"Talulah Gosh are going to go very 'girl group'. Kind of Shangri Las meets the Ramones" — Amelia Fletcher, in 53rd and 3rd *fanzine, '86.*

Elizabeth Price of Talulah Gosh / '86
An early live shot at White Horse,
Brixton.

Left: Talulah Gosh / '86
Peter Momtchiloff, Chris Scott, Matthew Fletcher, Elizabeth Price, Amelia Fletcher. Shot originally used on rear sleeve of the "Beatnik Boy" single, released on Stephen Pastel's 53rd and 3rd label.

Above: Talulah Gosh / '87
Eithne Farry (who filled Price's boots in '87), Amelia Fletcher, Matthew Fletcher and Chris Scott at Click Club, Birmingham.

Above: Amelia Fletcher and Eithne Farry / '87

Right: Peter Momtchiloff / '87

"Hey Ho! Let's Gosh, c'mon let's Gosh..."

Previous page: Lawrence of Felt / '86
Enigmatic bohemian style icon, Lawrence, formed Felt in
Birmingham and released ten singles and ten albums in ten
years between '79 and '89 on Cherry Red and Creation Records
respectively.

"I just wish my life could be as strange as a conspiracy
I hold out but there's no way of being what I want to be
Dragons blow fire angels fly spirits in the air
I'm just me I can't deny I'm neither here, there nor anywhere"
– From Felt's "Primitive Painters"

Left: Lawrence of Felt / '87
Live at Greenock Subterraneans.

Above: Sandy Fleming / '86
Photographer and guitarist in Hangman's Beautiful Daughters,
Sandy Fleming, took the photos used on Felt's "Poem of the River"
and TVP's "I Know Where Syd Barrett Lives" record sleeves.

Philip King of Felt / '86

Primal Scream's first single "All Fall Down" epitomises the Byrdsian, Love inspired wistful jangle sound that was beginning to engulf the UK indie scene in the mid '80s. It was recorded whilst singer Bobby Gillespie was still drumming for the JAMC. The follow-up's B side, "Velocity Girl", is seen by many as their indie pop era masterpiece and was included on the *NME*'s *C86* cassette compilation. Bobby Gillespie also became something of an indie-boy cult style icon at this time, contributing to the popularity of mid-'60s sartorial elements in the indie youth scenes.

Previous page: Primal Scream / '86
Martin St John, James Beattie, Bobby Gillespie, Thomas McGurk, Paul Harte, Robert Young. Live at Room at the Top, London.

Above: Bobby Gillespie / '87

Right: Primal Scream / '85
Live at the Clarendon, Hammersmith, London.

Bobby Gillespie / '85
Live at Ziggy's Plymouth. With Jeff Barrett on the right, who owned a local record shop at the time called Meat Whiplash, after the Fire Engines' song.

14 Iced Bears / '86
Kevin Canham, Dominic Mills, Nick Emery and Robert Sekula.
Brighton's psychedelic troubadours, 14 Iced Bears, were inspired
by The West Coast Pop Art Experimental Band and the 13th Floor
Elevators. Led by Rob Sekula, 14 Iced Bears were on numerous
labels including Frank Records, run by Mark Flunder, and the
cultish Sarah Records.

Heralding from West Bromwich, The Sea Urchins personify the '80s/'60s indie youth crossover style – going for the all out anorak attack. They also hold the enviable title of being the first band to be released on the mythological Sarah Records. The "Pristine Christine" single is regarded as one of the jewels in the crown of UK '80s indie pop and commands mind boggling sums these days. I wish I'd bought a copy when it was £1.99! Live at the Mermaid in Birmingham.

The Sea Urchins / '86
Robert Cooksey, James Roberts, Bridget Duffy, Simon Woodcock, Mark Bevin.

Previous page left: James Roberts / '87

Previous page right: Simon Woodcock / '87

Above: The Sea Urchins / '86
At the Click Club at Burberry's in Birmingham.

"The single title "Pristine Christine" was a reference to Robert's mum continually tidying up, but the song is not about her. Clothes were from the rag market in Birmingham, jumble sales and charity shops. A little vintage shop called Razor's Edge always had a great selection of anoraks – I think The Pastels had a lot to do with the anorak explosion, although at the time I was channeling a '60s car crash look mashing up Dusty, Rita Tushingham, kitchen sink '60s chic…. I met Robert and James via Hugh as they were looking for a drummer… I was rubbish at the audition but a striped Cathy McGowan coat won them over… The whole indie scene was a retreat from the hi-gloss veneer of the '80s – all the over-polished pop stars and music – punk DIY attitude with '60s attire made for a far more exciting prospect." – Bridget Duffy

Lenny Helsing of The Green Telescope / '84
Way cool Edinburgh garage/ DIY/acid punk combo The Green
Telescope were easily the finest '60s garage band from the UK
in the '80s. Note Lenny's Woolies-esque cheapo guitar with VOX
lettering stuck on.

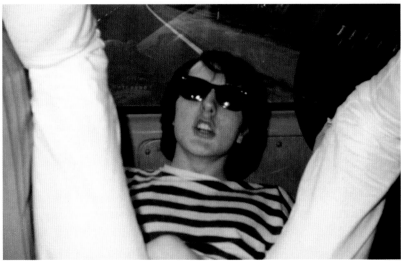

Top: Pooh Sticks and Amelia Fletcher / '88
Katie Courtney-Jones, Huw Williams and post-Talulah Gosh Amelia
Fletcher, who made some cameos for the Pooh Sticks at the time.

Bottom: Paul (Pabs) Phillips of the Pooh Sticks / '88

Right: Pooh Sticks / '88
Paul (Pabs) Phillips and Huw Williams, the Welsh John's Children,
in full "Orgasm" pop art freakout mode

My Bloody Valentine
A reflection by David Conway, founding member of My Bloody Valentine

Strangely enough it was exactly 30 years ago that I first met Kevin Shields and Colm Ó Cíosóig, after I'd replied to an advertisement placed by then bass player, Mark Ross, in a Dublin record shop. The music scene in Dublin was extremely conservative and stifling at the time – the primary influence that deposited a rather large Bono-shaped turd in the communal punch bowl was, of course, U2. I tend to regard the Virgin Prunes as providing the most significant gleam of light (and darkness) to illuminate the otherwise drab and dismal wilderness of casually calculated conformity that constituted the creative cul-de-sac that was the Dublin music scene at that time.

Given this grim landscape, it is impossible to overstate the significance of the emergent gothic scene both in terms of press coverage and the response of fans and new bands. In 1983 it seemed to be everywhere – at least as far as the music magazines reported it – and paradoxically nowhere in terms of anything one might consider a tangible physical presence. Goth in those days meant something rather different then than it does now. For a start, it was far less homogeneous and rigidly defined before it achieved its zenith. Its origins were a kind of progression from the style then referred to as 'positive punk', a kind of bass-heavy,

reverb-drenched sound that generally featured jagged shards of brittle guitar and dramatic vocals, the most well-known proponents being bands like UK Decay, The Sex Gang Children and Southern Death Cult.

The impact of the gothic scene at the time as far as the fledgling My Bloody Valentine was concerned was considerable, and the one band, rather tenuously associated with the style, that stood not so much head and shoulders but on an entirely different level above all the rest, was the Birthday Party. From a personal perspective at least, it is impossible to underestimate their influence – from both a musical point of view as well as in terms of aesthetics and style. I know these days, it's probably considered something of a sacrilege to include the Birthday Party with any of the young pretenders to the gothic crown of thorns coveted by so many would-be princes of darkness, but it helps illustrate the point that the scene was rather more diverse at the time. Their motifs of faith and violence, despair and redemption, the macabre and the grotesque had their roots in the tradition of the Southern Gothic style.

My personal style choices at this time tended towards a suit or jacket and trousers ensemble with a shirt and optional tie – mostly dark colours or the obligatory black – and

My Bloody Valentine / '86
David Conway, Debbie Googe, Colm Ó Cíosóig, Kevin Shields.

contrived a lurid kaleidoscope of low-budget/ high-concept delirium, a day-glow nightmare of ecstasy viewed through 3-D glasses in the murky subterranean twilight where precocious arthouse pretension goes slumming with – and is effortlessly seduced by – the taboo glamour of unrepentant pop trash. The impact of this particular vision encouraged us to appreciate how being in this kind of band might potentially be fun.

In 1984 we toured around Holland and later West Berlin, and the main influence we began to absorb both as a band and as individuals was what is generally described as garage-punk. Among the most visible exponents of this particular style at the time in Holland were The Nomads, The Lyres and The Scientists. The latter had the most decisive influence upon how the MBV style was starting to develop. We could relate to The Scientists' nod to the looks and sounds of groups like The Stooges and MC5. It wasn't that they were simply adopting a kind of psychedelic/hippy retro image, but seemed instead to be employing certain aspects of that style in a way that also acknowledged and incorporated elements of glam and punk.

One other group I believe played a significant role in band's development was The Gun Club. The band was extremely popular in Europe at the time. In terms of their image and sound they represented a nexus where various past and future styles overlapped. Jeffrey Lee Pierce's idiosyncratic look, vocals and blues-punk stylings, coupled with the presence of Kid Congo Powers, who would later play with The Cramps, and Patricia Morrison on bass, crystallized a subversive and powerful yet extremely accessible synthesis of the various influences prevalent at the time, all of which they made uniquely their own.

MBV's debut mini-LP, *This is Your Bloody Valentine*, was recorded within a fortnight of our arrival in West Berlin, a city that fulfilled

winklepicker shoes or Chelsea boots. I sported a bird's nest of fairly long back-combed hair, a mutation of the style I'd originally adopted when I first got into punk. At this point there was no real attempt to 'formalise' a look or image for the band. The three of us – myself, Kevin and Colm – who constituted the nucleus of the band, sort of drifted into looking a particular way that was really just an extension of how we individually looked at the time.

Even though I've placed particular emphasis on the significance of the gothic scene on the development of what would eventually become My Bloody Valentine's visual style, we were already – both individually and as a group – drawing on a wider variety of musical and stylistic influences. Many of these are probably the obvious and rather predictable ones – The Doors, the Velvet Underground, The Stooges and the Ramones, as well as experimental bands like Einsturzende Neubauten, Foetus, SPK and Test Department. Another group from that time that are also worth mentioning were The Cramps. The Cramps inhabited, celebrated and epitomised a sensationalistic grindhouse world the title of their second studio album captured perfectly, *Psychedelic Jungle*. Their records and live performances our overly romantic hopes of what it might be. It serves as a document of the band's tentative and, at times, faltering steps towards self-realisation. The group photograph on the front cover and the individual portraits on the reverse sleeve accurately represent a band whose members are not entirely on the same page as far as image and style are concerned. This aesthetic conflict is reflected by the music – an awkward hybridisation of punk/garage/rockabilly/psychedelic tropes filtered through an obscure, goth-clouded lens.

MBV arrived in London separately in April/May 1985, and after a brief stint of homelessness, finally reunited in the Finsbury Park area at which point Christine Durkin, who had been on keyboards, left the band and Deb Googe joined as bass player. With this line-up we began rehearsing in earnest at Salem Studios in Euston, which was also headquarters of Fever Records, who would eventually release our first EP in this country.

It became apparent to us – even prior to our arrival – that the most significant development on the UK scene was the emergence of Creation Records and their most celebrated alumni, the Jesus and Mary Chain. Anyone familiar with the history of MBV would be in no doubt as to the significant influence the JAMC had over the band's subsequent development. But, while this is undeniable and demonstrably true, their impact didn't quite represent a path of uninterrupted linear progression as far as MBV were concerned. Although the current official history of that period often creates the impression that the entire Creation Records roster bestrode the indie scene like behemoths, casually brushing aside any supposed competition to win the hearts and minds of the nation's pop kids, the truth was actually a little different. The 'scene' was very fragmented and probably experiencing the last spasmodic paroxysms of the tribalism once so typical of youth culture. Things weren't quite as homogeneous/harmonious in terms of a general pop consensus in favour of the new-fangled jangly sound so fondly remembered today. Let's not forget that *NME*'s infamous *C86*, though now synonymous with the sounds of say, Primal Scream's "Velocity Girl", The Shop Assistants and the Pastels et al, was simply the name of the cassette, which also featured the likes of Stump, Bogshed and Age of Chance, who could never be described as, well, 'shambling' or 'jangly'.

The most visible manifestation of the pop subculture at this point was the looming, omnipresent spectre of goth. At the time, The Sisters of Mercy were headlining at the Royal Albert Hall, and The Cult (having incrementally shed the presumably superfluous encumberances of their former prefixes, 'Southern' and 'Death') were busy flexing their stadium rock muscles. For a band with a name like My Bloody Valentine, the overwhelming primacy of this highly-visible goth scene posed something of a problem. Of course, we might have capitalised on the initially ambiguous – but now decidedly misleading – name, and simply taken the path of least resistance down a more conventional goth-tinged route. But none of us – even me, generally (if not unanimously) considered the worst offender in this regard – had much appetite for that. For a brief period we came to consider the name such a potential millstone that we seriously considered changing it, but for some reason lacked the collective wit or imagination to come up with an alternative.

As a result, the idea of looking as different to anything that might be considered 'goth' suddenly assumed an unprecedented urgency. The primary focus at that time became the all-consuming issue of coiffure. Since we had already been immersing ourselves in various psychedlic and garage-pop influences, primarily of a '65-'69 vintage, the adoption of the characteristic 'bowl-head' haircut seemed entirely logical. Adopting that style had not only the immediate advantage of separating us from a scene we didn't want to associate with, but also had the added bonus of creating an immediately identifiable group image.

Once we had taken the quite calculated and deliberate step of immersing our individual selves within this communal hive identity, the idea of recasting the band as a kind of cartoon became strangely irresistible. The initial influence of the Ramones – Kevin was an especially avid fan – resurfaced. We were listening to more and more to music that was melodically orientated and unashamedly pop driven; the Kinks, the Byrds the Beatles (the Rubber Soul/Revolver period predominantly), The Who, The Monkees and even Dusty Springfield. The general revamp of MBV's image and emerging musical style was formalised as a concept with the *Geek!* EP, recorded in October '85 and released by Fever Records in May '86. In fact the title 'Geek!' essentially came about as a deliberate reference to how, well, geeky we looked and a rather perverse determination to cultivate the image even further.

In the hiatus between recording and releasing *Geek!* the whole issue of the band's evolving identity assumed a greater urgency and impetus. We were starting to play quite regularly in and around London as well as playing a short tour in Holland and Germany, and the responses we were getting still placed a rather undue emphasis on the more – for want of a better expression – rock aspects of our style. This assessment accelerated the process of reinvention and a kind of Jacobin-style wardrobe purge commenced. Obviously colours and fabrics were rigorously scrutinised in terms of what they might appear to represent. Black – the sombre shade so beloved of rock n' rollers, beatniks, goths, Catholic priests and, uh, Nazis

– came in for special consideration. Though not entirely dismissed out of hand, black was regarded in terms of context – something to be worn in combination rather than comprising an entire ensemble. Leather was also contentious – not just with the members of MBV but within the scene itself – embraced by the likes of JAMC, The Weather Prophets and Primal Scream, and reviled by others as a return to 'the unacceptable face of rockism'. As far as MBV were concerned leather became more or less verboten.

When it came to jackets too, there were soul-searching decisions to be made. Here leather was actually considered fine, along with suede and corduroy – and the style du jour was the plain and unadorned three-quarter length. As far as shoes were concerned, I'd always been fond of winklepickers, Chelsea boots and even Cuban heels. One of the premier establishments in London at the time was Johnson's the Modern Outfitters – created by Lloyd Johnson – who had a shop upstairs at Kensington Market, which boasted a really impressive collection of very stylish footwear. Of course, I was generally broke in those days, so I could very rarely afford to lay out any cash on such upscale merchandise. However, I do recall picking up a pair of charcoal grey Chelsea boots from Johnson's the Modern Outfitters in '86, simply because they matched the faux python skin trousers I'd also bought at Kensington Market. Thinking about it now, I suspect myself and Christine, who also bought a very cool pair of boots in the same store that day were probably spending the rent money; but you could get away with that sort of thing then – well, at least where we lived. We were all fairly broke, but it was easy to pick up all sorts of things from places like Kensington Market, our local Nag's Head Market in Holloway and even Camden Market. Charity shops were pretty good then too. Consider that the '80s liked to promote itself as the 'designer decade', I guess that we were making a stance against that particular doctrine too – albeit in a subconscious way and one that was largely borne of financial necessity.

By '86, the changing look and sound of MBV was so noticeable that in a live review for the NME Dave Jennings wrote: "The sight and sound of My Bloody Valentine welcomes one in a parallel universe where the Jesus and Mary Chain paid more attention to Wayne Fontana and the Mindbenders than the Velvet Underground." That year, we played gigs in all sorts of venues – from tiny spaces like upstairs at the Enterprise, Chalk Farm, to larger stages such as The Timebox promoted by Jon 'Fat' Beast at the Bull and Gate Kentish Town – and with so many bands that it's impossible to remember them all – The Young Gods, The Primitives, Talulah Gosh, The Shop Assistants, The Soup Dragons, Pop Will Eat Itself, The Wolfhounds.... The cumulative result of all this activity and stylistic reinvention was that by the time we came to record the (not so imaginatively titled) EP *The New Record by My Bloody Valentine* for Joe Foster's Kaleidoscope Sound label in late summer '86, we'd more less coalesced as a group with an identifiable sound and image that the record itself quite accurately reflected.

Anyway, that just about covers everything I can think of. I'm sure the other members of MBV might well remember it all quite differently. I guess memories like these are by their very nature subject to the obscure currents sometimes called 'stream of consciousness'... maybe it's a case of Pop Traumatic Stress Disorder. Thinking about it now, your humble narrator certainly seemed to spend most of the period in question in an almost permanent hypnagogic trance state... which, all things considered, was probably the most effective survival strategy to have adopted during the '80s. And now, if you'll excuse me, following that extended glimpse into the indie-pop abyss, it's time for a nice cup of tea and a little lie down...

Be seeing you!

Clippings from David Conway's archive

Previous page: My Bloody Valentine / '86
David Conway, Kevin Shields, Unknown, Colm Ó Cíosóig standing in front of the Berlin Wall during a Germany/Denmark tour.

"During those engagements the Chernobyl nuclear reactor went critical and the resulting cloud of radioactive fallout seemed to follow us from one gig to the other both in Germany and Denmark."
— David Conway

Above: Colm Ó Cíosóig and Debbie Googe / '86

Right: Debbie Googe / '86
University gig, London.

Left: Kevin Shields / '83
Kevin performing at the very first MBV gig, 17th August '83, Dublin.

Above: MBV fan / '87
Outside Speed Club, London.

Overleaf: MBV / '86
David Conway, Kevin Shields, Debbie Googe, Colm Ó Cíosóig.

I first noticed My Bloody Valentine after reading a small feature in an '86 issue of *Sounds*. The band's visual instantly grabbed me – they looked exactly like I did at that time with bowl haircuts, grotty '60s leather box jackets and skinny black jeans mixups. Their new EP, *Geek*, on the Fever label was described as a "very loud melodic drone". I was intrigued. The following weekend I embarked on a regular pilgrimage to Portobello Road to wander around the flea market and visit the holy ground that was Plastic Passion, easily the best record shop that's ever existed in London and a gathering/meeting place of the bowl cut youth garage/indie tribes on any given Saturday afternoon. Obscuro collector boffin types browsed the new releases/re-releases as well as the mind boggling array of '60s originals and scarce new wave/punk era artifacts that were achieving cult status.

With my slim record buying budget I picked a reissue copy of the *Missing Links* LP on Raven, a Crimson Shadows 45, *New England Teen Scene vol. 2* comp and a shot in the dark with the MBV *Geek* EP with a lurid orange sleeve, higgledy piggledy lettering and distorted pic of the band. It looked cool, and the guy in the shop said it was really shitty, sounding like a third rate *Psychedelic Jungle* era Cramps and the first JAMC single, in other words mandatory… I was sold. Returning later to my bedroom in Leigh-on-Sea I put the record on, following instructions on the back to play loud and to turn the treble up. I did so at maximum volume as the swampy dirge of "No Place To Go" filled the room. Lying on the floor staring at the ceiling whilst enjoying a rollup I was absorbed in total Geekdom! SK

Above: MBV / '86
Live at the Bull and Gate, Kentish Town, London.

Right: MBV fans / '86

Left: Bilinda Butcher of MBV / '88
Exit Dave Conway after *Sunny Sundae Smile* EP, enter Bilinda
Butcher. New line-up, new sound. Live at Leeds Poly.

Above: Bilinda Butcher and Debbie Googe / '88

Above: Kevin Shields / '87

Right: MBV / '87
Debbie, Bilinda and Colm play at Portlands, London. Shot taken
around the time of the *Strawberry Wine* EP, the first MBV release
after Conway's departure.

Spacemen 3 / '87
Peter Kember (Sonic Boom), Jason Pierce, Pete (Bassman) Bains,
Sterling (Rosco) Roswell. Pioneering minimalist psychedelic
outsider dronesters from Rugby, Spacemen 3 were without doubt
one of the most extraordinarily original and mind altering groups
the UK has ever produced. Performing live whilst seated and rarely
acknowledging the audience, they exuded the antithesis of any
vile "rockist" exhibitionism. Pure concentration projecting an
overwhelming sonic assault capable of leveling buildings to their
humble foundations.

Overleaf left: Spacemen 3 / '86
Clockwise from top left: Natty Brooker, Bassman, Jason and Sonic.
This shot is an outtake from the cover shoot of the *Walking with
Jesus* EP, which obscured the band using an oil projection.

Overleaf right: Peter Kember (Sonic) / '87

Left: Spacemen 3 / '87

Overleaf left: Spacemen 3 / '87
Clockwise from top left: Pete Bain, Sterling 'Rosco' Roswell,
Pete Kember, Jason Pierce. Live at the Leeds Packhouse.

Overleaf right: Pete Kember and Jason Pierce / '87
Shot used for *The Perfect Prescription* LP on Glass Records.

I first encountered Loop quite by surprise at Bay 63 in Ladbroke Grove some time in '86. Myself and a couple of pals, namely Ian and Patsie, had made the trip up from Southend to see The Pastels, and Loop turned out to be the support. Between pulsating waves of fuzz and feedback, the group voyaged through a set of tremulous numbers in a hallucinogenic repetitive style (repetitive in a positive way a la Suicide, Scientists), systematically zoning out the floppy fringed youths in the crowd. SK

Above: Robert Hampson of Loop / '86
Robert displaying '80s indie boy chic with distinct '60s garage leanings. Black Chelsea boots, skinny black jeans and black jumper (often a roll neck) became de riguer for the UK's Velvets obsessed youths during the mid/late '80s. At Bay 63, Ladbroke Grove, London.

Right: Robert Hampson / '86

Overleaf: Loop / '86
Robert Hampson, Becky Stewart (Bex), James Endeacott, Glen Ray. An early Loop set live at Douglas Hart of JAMC's Speed Club in London.

Left: Loop with Bex / '88
Robert Hampson, John Wills and Neil MacKay with Bex of Sun
Carriage and unspecified cat.

Above: Bex and Mash (Matthew Watts) of Sun Carriage /'88

Market Memoirs;
A conversation with
Lloyd Johnson

It's impossible to discuss '80s underground music's visual sound without citing Lloyd Johnson and his sartorial youth mecca emporium, Johnson's the Modern Outfitters, in Kensington Market and on The King's Road.

SK: Kensington Market; you were there from beginning to end, and no shopping experience has come close since. What do you think gave that particular market its unique energy?

LJ: Patrick Cockell and I opened in Kensington Market because John Dacie and Ian Lockhead who managed Just Men in Chelsea were mates of ours.... They told us about this place with shops within a huge store. We didn't understand what they were talking about... that didn't exist until Kensington Market happened... so we went along and had a look and decided to take a stall in there. We were given a piece of chalk and told to mark out the area we wanted on the floor – the place was a empty shell. We went to the wood yard and bought some wood and plaster board and built our stall... that's the way it was done in the beginning of the market.

SK: Your store was a Mecca for young music fans and musicians spanning three decades. What do you think that your store offered to keep such fickle clientele loyal and satisfied for so long?

LJ: All my ideas came from my youth experience of seeing bands on Hastings Pier and of my mod days in Hastings. I have a very visual memory... when we did second hand clothing in the '70s, before it was known as vintage, I got to know what styles sold the best second hand-wise. When the really good stuff seemed to be drying up, we went for '20s, '30s, '40s, '50s, '60s fabrics... there were still plenty of old fabrics knocking around up north... so we made our glamourised versions of the good second hand stuff from the '40s, '50s and '60s... I thought of us as a youth culture/rock 'n roll shop...

SK: You are the master of taking rock 'n roll energy and converting it into fashion without losing any of its raw authenticity. I am assuming you are a big music fan... can you tell me about your influences?

LJ: Various stage outfits from bands of the '50s and '60s are imprinted in my mind, so they just pop up when I start thinking of ideas. The coffin changing rooms in the shop in the '70s were inspired by Screaming Lord Sutch... the basement of the King's Road shop was inspired by '60s Hammer Horror films... it just seemed right to go into a gloomy basement and find it covered with cobwebs and Sweeney Todd's barber chair sitting there.

SK: From '79 onwards there was a huge '60s revival. Many artists from this period cite your store as the place they got key elements of their look from. Did this shift in music give you a second wave of sales? Were you selling these new kids the same styles you had sold in the '60s?

    LJ: We just did what we wanted to do... it wasn't planned... if we found some great fabrics we'd just say "that would look great made into such and such...". People weren't aware that I had started in 1966, or that I'd had a previous life with Cockell and Johnson from '67 to '73, which was an extension of a mod/French/dandy look....

SK: Your footwear in particular was popular with everyone from punks, mods, indie kids and so on. What do you think was the source of this appeal?

    LJ: I have always had fond memories of the windows of Winter's shoe shop in George Street, Hastings during the late '50s and early '60s. They sold Denson Personality Shoes.... I have a collection of their style catalogues, which were a constant source of inspiration.

SK: You always seemed to be one step ahead. What gave you such foresight into the next youth/music zeitgeist?

    LJ: I don't think the term 'one step ahead' applies if you are just doing what

you want to do, if you understand what I mean.... It's like enjoying running on your own... it's not until you look behind you that you realise you are in a race and there are a lot of people following you/copying you. At times some REAL INDIVIDUALS would appear and inspire things. That's what happened with the Japanese range we did. A friend was managing The Pretenders at the time and was a collector of clothing etc from the war in the Pacific.... He showed me a photo of a 19-year-old pilot who looked amazing and that set that one off.

SK: As a 16-year-old in '84 I remember entering the Kensington Market store and hearing the Cramps playing. My jaw dropped, thinking "wow! I'm walking into a whole new world". The music seemed to go hand in hand with the clothes. Who put together the soundtrack to your store?

    LJ: A lot of the staff also did DJ nights so there was a friendly appreciation of music... they were in charge of the music. I just wanted them to be happy and get on with their jobs of keeping the place clean tidy and selling clothes. They'd all go to the clubs and know most of the customers as friends... we had great staff. There were three or four great New Year's Eve parties at The Venue in Victoria where bands that were customers would play for free.

SK: I have been involved in some nostalgic conversations wishing we could get our hands on some Chelsea boots today.... Would you consider re-issuing a few Johnsons shoe styles for old times' sake?

    LJ: Look up 'La Rocka! 79' on the net... we are doing a few bits and pieces at a leisurely pace....

Previous page: Loop scenesters / '88
Backstage in Glasgow.

Above: Norman Blake of the Clouds / '87
Norman was a prolific musician, who moonlighted between
numerous bands including The Pastels, the Pretty Flowers (later to
become the BMX Bandits), Boy Hairdressers and the Clouds. Shot in
Martin Whitehead's flat in Bath, home of Subway Records.

Right: Clouds / '87
Norman Blake, John Charnley, Gino Lonta, Bill Charnley, Andy Brady.
Short-lived cool Glasgow teen jingle janglers.

Previous page left, top: The Wylde Things / '86
Chris Jordan, Philip Marriott, Hugh Dellar, Louis Wiggett,
Peter Kemp. The huge slew of '60s garage/beat reissues and
compilations a la *Back from the Grave, Transworld Punk,*
etc, that flooded the market throughout the '80s had a deep
impact on kids all over, even reaching provincial Rye in East
Sussex in the shape of the Wylde Things, Sussex's answer to
the Keggs and Selfkick.

Previous page left, bottom: Clouds / '87

Previous page right: John Wills / '86
Drummer from The Servants and Loop.

172

Left: Flesh / '87
Flesh, Welsh indie unknowns, had the last word in bowl cut barnets.
The Pooh Sticks used this image for their "On Tape" single sleeve,
released on Fierce Records. It was taken in the toilets of a club in
Port Talbot on the night Primal Scream were playing.

Above: The Servants / '85
John Mohan and Philip King in Brighton.

Previous page: BMX Bandits / '87
Norman Blake, Francis Macdonald, Billy Woods, Duglas T Stewart,
Jim McCulloch and Joe McAlinden in Bellshill.

*"Norman Blake, Sean Dickson and I weren't typical boys from
Bellshill. We didn't fit in to the Bellshill way of doing things or
seeing the world. First of all we found strength in finding each
other and then we found others who didn't fit in in their towns.
Together we grew stronger, until we were strong enough to go our
own ways and find our own paths." – Duglas T Stewart, founding
member of the BMX Bandits*

Above left: BMX Bandits / '86
In Glasgow.

Above right: Duglas T Stewart / '87

Previous page left: Jim Lambie of the Boy Hairdressers / '87
Short-lived group from Belshill, who released one enchantingly melodious and melancholic EP, *Golden Shower*, on 53rd and 3rd before three of its members metamorphasised into Teenage Fanclub.

Previous page right: Joe McAlinden and Raymond McGinlay of the Boy Hairdressers / '87

Above: Joe McAlinden / '87

Right: Norman Blake of the Boy Hairdressers/ '87

Above: The Pastels and the Vaselines / '87
The two bands on tour; Alasdair (the driver), Frances McKee
(Vaselines) and Annabel Wright (aka Aggi of The Pastels).

Right top: The Pastels and the Vaselines / '87
Martin Hayward (The Pastels) Eugene Kelly, Charlie Kelly
(Vaselines).

Right bottom: The Pastels and the Vaselines / '87
Brian Taylor (The Pastels) Charlie Kelly (Vaselines).

Largely overlooked during their relatively brief lifetime, Glasgow's indie pop sensations the Vaselines became a household name a couple of years after they'd broken up when Nirvana covered one of their songs, "Molly's Lips". Allegedly Kurt Cobain described Kelly and McKee as his "most favorite songwriters in the world".

Above: Vaselines / '87
Charlie Kelly, Eugene Kelly and Frances McKee

Right: Frances McKee and Eugene Kelly / '87

Above and left: Vaselines / '86
Early live shots, whilst still a duo in Glasgow.

Overleaf left: *The Cut* **/ '87**
An early interview with the Vaselines in this Scottish music paper.

Overleaf right: Frances McKee and Eugene Kelly / '87

SLIPPERY CUSTOMERS

THEY ARE a calculatedly ingenious pair, these **Vaselines**. Why, I am attempting to ask them, did a certain music journalist say such steamily excited things about you and your soon-to-be-released 53rd and 3rd debut waxing in his recent articlette?

"I hate exclamation marks," exclaims Eugene. "He said we weren't glorifying sex and living dirty when I think we are."

"*Rory Rides Me Raw* on the single's 'B' side has the line *Rory ride me slowly, ride me raw, raw, raw*," says Frances brightly. "Rory is the name of my bicycle so that's that answered. It's the alliteration as well," she adds in a primly helpful tone.

"If people want to misinterpret our songs as being about sex, that's up to them - it's not our fault," says Eugene.

But aren't you trying to subvert contemporary moves, comment obliquely on 'eighties self-centredness and suchlike?

"We don't want to subvert anybody. Nice pop ditties is what it is... but if people see us as introducing sex in indie scene, we

The Vaselines were born out of the duos' fanzine, "Which would have been called either *Pure Fucking Crap* or *D Dull And Boring* had we bothered to leave the pub for long enough to write it, but we never

The Vaselines describe their music as "Euro! Disco! Rock!" The singles' 'A' side, *Son Of A Gun* is a subtle(ish) r to Divine's *Shoot Your Shot*. Divine's *So You Think You're A Man* receives aural Vaselining on the 'B' side; a very fa tremendously sexy Scottish rock superstar moans breathily on the chorus. I say that I'm sure it's Jim Kerr - is Eugene and Frances loo

Eugene would like to be the new Kelly-Marie. Frances says that "For years people have been studying poetr turning all its sense into crap: we are the reverse of that process, crap into se

They are currently looking for musicians with which to form a band, "Someone who can't play the guitar too we who hasn't got much time on their hands... someone who'll go down the pub after a gig. And before. And d Someone who can talk a good gig in the

Their message to the world is: "If you see us lying in the gutter, pick us up and put us back in the pub."

Photography credits

Front Cover – James Finch

Page 2 – contributed by Sam Knee, photographer unknown

Pages 6, 7 , 8, 9, 11, 12, 14, 25 top, 26, 28, 29 – Peter McArthur

Pages 10, 63, 66, 68, 71, 72, 73, 78, 88, 89, 91, 168, 169, 170 bottom – Martin Whitehead

Page 13 – Roxanne New

Page 15 – Angus Whyte

Pages 16-17 – Paul Rosen

Pages 18, 19 bottom, 32, 33, 36, 37, 42, 43, 86, 87, 114, 115, 120, 121, 184, 185 – Mark Flunder

Page 19 top – Pat Bermingham

Pages 20, 142, 144, 145 – Ken Kopsey

Page 22 – contributed by Julian Leusby, photographer unknown

Page 23 – contributed by Lenny Helsing, photography by Robin Gillanders

Page 24 – contributed by John Robb, photography by Ian Tilton

Page 25 bottom – Ian Bishop

Pages 30, 31 – Lawrence Watson

Pages 34, 35, 110 – Jim Barr

Page 40 – contributed by Simon Murphy

Page 41 – contributed by Stephen McRobbie photography by Annabel Wright

Pages 44, 45, 60, 62 108, 109 – JC Brouchard

Pages 46-47 – contributed by Chris Davidson, original illustration by George Millar

Pages 48, 49, 118, 119 – Valerie Hicks

Pages 50, 52 – Steve Cope

Pages 51, 53, 54, 59 – David Evans

Pages 55, 138, 139, 141, 158 – Nick Allport

Page 56 – Andrew Catlin

Pages 58, 76, 159, 160, 162, 163, 166 – James Finch

Pages 64, 65 – Innis McAllister

Page 70 – contributed by Susan Henderson

Pages 74, 112, 171, 173 – contributed by Philip King, photography by Sandy Fleming

Page 75 – Janet Knee

Page 77 – David Newton

Page 79 – Jon Hunter

Page 80 – contributed by Bob Collins, photography by Gail Lusted

Pages 82, 83 – contributed by Mick Geoghegan, photographer unknown

Pages 84, 85, back cover – contributed by Stephen McRobbie, photographer unknown

Pages 90, 117 – Dave Driscoll

Pages 92, 93 – Paul Reed

Pages 94,95 – Ross McIntyre

Pages 96, 97 – contributed by David Callahan, photography by Andrew Springham

Pages 100, 101, 102, 130 – Steve Double

Page 104 – permission for use from Talulah Gosh band member, photographer unknown

Pages 105, 126 – Dave Travis

Pages 106, 107 – Bob Barker

Page 111 – contributed by Philip King, photography by Danny Weinstein

Page 116 – Elinor Richter

Pages 122, 123 – Mick Geoghegan

Pages 124, 125 – Mark Hynds

Page 127 – contributed by Lenny Helsing, photography by Alan McLean

Pages 128 top, 129 – Paul Phillips

Page 128 bottom – Katie Courtney-Jones

Pages 132, 136, 140 – contributed by David Conway, photographer unknown

Pages 146, 147 – Alan Fairnie

Page 148 – Jo Brooks

Page 149 – contributed by Chip Fireball, photography by Beverley Castle

Pages 150, 152, 154, 157 – Craig Wagstaff

Page 153 – Heidi Schramli

Page 156 – Julian Gonnerman

Page 170 top – contributed by Hugh Dellar, photographer unknown

Page 172 – Steve Gregory

Pages 174, 176, 177 – contributed by Duglas T. Stewart, photography by Sharon Fitzgerald

Pages 178, 179, 180, 181– contributed by Joe McAlinden, photographer unknown

Pages 182, 183, 186, 187 – Stephen McRobbie

Page 188 – The Cut Scottish music paper article written by David Belcher, clipping contributed by Lenny Helsing, photography by Sharon Fitzgerald

Page 189 – Alastair Indge

Page 191 – Sarah Smith

About the Author

Sam Knee is an avid music fan, record nerd, musician on the peripheral outer limits with a brief stint in '87 with London garage band, The Mistreaters.

Vintage clothing aficionado, with 25 years trading and consulting under his anorak.

Menswear designer, specialising in bringing authentic styles back from the grave.

Creator and writer of seminal '60s / '80s music blog with sartorial leanings, *www.leadersofmen.blogspot.com.*

Historian in post-war fashion, music and youth culture scenes.

www.asceneinbetween.com

Sam Knee / '85
At home in Leigh-on-Sea.

Acknowledgements

Firstly I'd like to pay homage and send sincerest love to my soulmate, Lisa, for all her undying faith and devotion through this life and beyond.

Extra special thanks for the humbling generosity of the following individuals. Without their contributions this book wouldn't have gone beyond one of my foggy notions. Good to know that money doesn't make the world go round after all.

David Conway, Martin Whitehead, Stephen Pastel, Amelia Fletcher, Lenny Helsing, James Finch, Jill Bryson, Peter McArthur, Hugh Dellar, Mark Flunder, Lloyd Johnson, Ken Copsey, JC Brouchard, Ziggy for keeping it real, April for computer wizardry.

Cheers one and all for the digging, delving, smashing and tedious scanning. DIY punk's not dead.

Nick Allport, Martin Langshaw, Keg TVP's site, Joe McAlinden, Duglas T Stewart, Gina Davidson, Chris Davidson, David Driscoll, Bob Collins, Paul (Pabs) Phillips, Philip King, Steve Cope.

Apologies if you went to the bother of submitting but didn't make the cut, we received an avalanche of killer material which surpassed all our expectations and sadly the line had to be drawn somewhere. Don't take it personally.

Published by Cicada Books Limited

Text and picture research by Sam Knee
Art editor Lisa Kidner
Design by April
Photographs as credited

British Library Cataloguing-in-Publication Data.

A CIP record for this book is available from the
British Library.
ISBN: 978-1-908714-06-0

Cicada Books Limited
48 Burghley Road
London NW5 1UE

T: +44 207 209 2259
E: ziggy@cicadabooks.co.uk
W: www.cicadabooks.co.uk

Front Cover – James Finch
Back cover – contributed by Stephen
McRobbie, photographer unknown